A Special Gift To Every Young Woman

EMPOWERING

HER

MIND

Nurturing Mental Resilience in Women

DR. GRACE JEREMIAH

TABLE OF CONTENTS

INTRODUCTION

The importance of mental wellness in women cannot be overstated. Mental wellness is not just the absence of mental illness but the presence of positive mental health and resilience. Women's mental health is crucial to one's total happiness and well-being because it preserves our cognitive flexibility, emotional stability, and sense of balance in our personal lives, careers, and interpersonal connections. Good mental health is shown when a person is psychologically stable and at peace with themselves. Women's mental health is often conceived of in the context of a mental ailment like dementia, an anxiety disorder, or severe depression. The truth is that these two groups are significantly different from one another. Women's mental health is very important and should never be neglected.

Various forms of women's mental health exist, including:

Cognitive: Cognitive mental health is concerned with preserving brain functions that may improve memory, the capacity to retain knowledge, and reasoning.

Psychological: This refers to the capacity to adjust to changes in one's life, such as children moving out and leaving the house or selling the long-cherished home. One may encourage well-being by emphasizing the good aspects of these life-altering experiences.

Emotionally: Maintaining a healthy balance in one's daily life is essential for both personal and professional success. When one accepts that they are at peace with themselves, they are actively displaying good mental health and wellbeing.

Not everyone is aware of this, but a poor mental state may cause issues in one's relationships, job, and even spirituality. Without the person being aware of it, their mental health has the power to influence many aspects of daily life. It might be challenging to manage everything while still keeping excellent mental health when there are demanding life schedules and habits to follow. It is crucial to set aside time each and every day to concentrate on one's mental and physical health in order to achieve living a positive life. A good view and mindset are essential to a person's health, both physically and mentally, and they may naturally yield advantages for mental health. Spend some time today focusing on your mind, body, and spirit; the rewards will be great.

The phrase "empowerment" is often used when discussing how to inspire and encourage women. What does it really imply, though? *To strengthen and instill confidence in someone, particularly in regard to taking charge of their lives and standing up for their rights.* Does this imply that women are passively waiting to be granted power? The reply is a categorical no!

The moment has come to recognize the power we each have within us, to utilize it, and most importantly, to expand upon it. The way we empower ourselves is the most significant empowerment. Utilizing and expanding the authority women currently possess is crucial for advancing development. Women in leadership roles benefit everyone, as we've already said. In actuality, it is essential for social change, political stability, and economic development. Recognize your advantages, and don't be reluctant to play to them. Be confident in your talents and prepared to pursue your wildest aspirations. Take chances and put forth the effort to make them pay off. Be tenacious, assured, and brave. Don't only trust in yourself; also believe in the ladies around you if you want to maintain momentum. In order to inspire future generations to follow suit, it is our responsibility to fully realize the potential that is within us. Consider that these young ladies have the inner strength to bring about change in the world. They will, too. Women have made significant contributions to "dismantling" in a variety of fields, including politics, the entertainment business, and many others.

CHAPTER ONE

DEFINING MENTAL WELLNESS

It is easiest to comprehend the intricate link between mental health and sickness by seeing them as two distinct continuums. Approximately 85% of individuals on the planet do not have a mental disease that has been medically diagnosed, but due to constant stress, anxiety, loneliness, and other problems, they are not all "mentally well" or flourishing. On the other side, people with a mental condition who have been diagnosed may nevertheless have a moderate or positive level of mental wellbeing (such as having satisfying relationships, feeling content, or doing well at work). In addition to traditional treatment plans, practices that promote mental wellbeing are increasingly understood to be protective factors for our mental health as well as aiding in reducing the intensity and symptoms of mental disease. Positive mental health is referred to as mental wellbeing. There is more to it than just being mentally well.

On one level, maintaining mental wellbeing is all about being proactive, dealing with life's challenges, and having the fortitude to handle stress, anxiety, loneliness, anger, and despair. On another level, mental health helps us progress toward a fuller, more meaningful human experience, which is sometimes referred to as thriving. The definition of what it means to thrive is arbitrary and individualized, and it is influenced by personal values, culture, religion, and beliefs. It could imply self-transcendence for one individual while it might mean operating at the top of their game and attaining their life objectives. Even while the mental health community has worked hard to reduce the stigma associated with mental illness, individuals in communities and cultures all over the globe still suffer from feelings of shame, denial, and secrecy.

Instead of merely avoiding or managing disease, mental health may help us change our attention to a more optimistic and powerful attitude (how we can feel, think, connect, and operate better). It highlights our ability to become more resilient, lessen pain, discover inner pleasure and serenity, and pursue meaning, connection, and other basic human desires. To deal with common mental and emotional difficulties like stress, burnout, loneliness, and unhappiness, people sorely need non-clinical, non-pathologizing coping mechanisms. Evidence suggests that enhancing our mental health might even lower our chance of contracting a mental disease, however worldwide, mental illness prevention and mental wellness promotion get insufficient attention.

The concept of mental wellness acknowledges the comprehensive and interwoven nature of our health and wellbeing. Our physical and mental states are linked with one another. We sometimes need to adjust our habits or techniques to cope with stress, build resilience, and overcome adversity when our circumstances change. The four primary routes of exercise and creativity, development and nutrition, rest and rejuvenation, and connection and meaning are used in this research to categorize the important techniques for mental wellbeing. Together, they constitute a range of possibilities for seeking mental wellbeing; there is no predetermined course to follow, and individuals may choose the tactics and pursuits that are most significant to or efficient for them.

CHAPTER TWO

THE GENDER PERSPECTIVE

According to studies, inequalities in mental health, health-seeking behavior of individuals afflicted, and reactions of the health system and society as a whole are caused by socially constructed variations in duties and responsibilities, status, and power between men and women. It is essential to bear in mind that there are important gaps while reviewing the study that has been done. Some mental health issues, including depression and schizophrenia, have male-female distinctions that are better studied than other situations. The situation in industrialized nations is more understood than the situation in developing countries, and adult men and women are better understood than children and adolescents.

The use of mental health services is divided by gender. Men are less likely than women to visit mental health professionals. Gender disparities are more pronounced in general care, while they are less pronounced in expert or residential care. It is not possible to attribute the gap in mental health care consumption between men and women to a lack of need. Men and women have distinct symptoms, even if there are no differences in the total frequency of psychopathology between the sexes. Women are more likely to have internalizing disorders than males are to experience externalizing ones. Only a small number of hypotheses on gender differences have been empirically evaluated.

Teenage females are far more likely than teenage boys to have depression, eating disorders, and suicide thoughts and attempts. Teenage guys are more prone than teenage girls to struggle with their emotions, participate in risky conduct, and even commit suicide. Teenage females are more prone than young boys to have symptoms that are inwardly focused. In adulthood, depression and anxiety are much more common in women than in men, although drug use disorders and antisocial conduct are more common in males. Due to genetic and biological reasons, women also tend to experience depression and anxiety disorders more often. Studies have shown a connection between mood swings and hormonal changes that occur throughout the menstrual cycle. Prenatal and postnatal depression risk increases as a consequence of the interaction of psychological and hormonal variables. Reproductive health problems may also cause severe psychological distress and difficulties in women. Hysterectomy and infertility are associated with a higher incidence of emotional and neurotic disorders in women.

Gender differences, according to social constructionist viewpoints, are actively (re)produced in social interactions rather than being in the person. It is societal notions of femininity and masculinity, not role identities or psychological traits, that influence how men and women think and behave. People consistently work to create the impression that men and women behave differently during social interactions because they have similar notions about what is appropriate conduct. Individuals with mental health problems perceive discomfort in different ways and seek help in different ways depending on their gender. Numerous studies have indicated that, compared to men, women reported greater levels of discomfort and were more likely to think they had an emotional condition.

Asking for aid, caring for one's health, and expressing one's emotions are all portrayed as feminine qualities. Men are supposed to be emotionally stable and to carry themselves with strength, independence, and dependability. In order to fit into the socially assigned masculine role, males are therefore urged to identify themselves in contrast to women by hiding their own health requirements and declining to get treatment. Because of this gendered role conflict, men may be reluctant to seek professional assistance and may worry that doing so would make them more stigmatized. When it comes to therapy, males are more likely than women to opt to handle mental illness on their own. Men tend to choose a quick and simple answer if they do decide to seek expert assistance. They thus choose medical care over psychotherapy more often than women do.

CHAPTER THREE

COMMON MENTAL HEALTH CHALLENGES IN WOMEN

There are several mental health conditions that affect women more often. Some mental health issues affect women more often than males and may have a big impact on how well they are overall. While males are more likely to have autism, early-onset schizophrenia, antisocial personality disorder, and alcoholism, women are more likely to have the following mental health conditions:

Depression: Women are twice as likely as men to experience depression (12 percent of women experience it compared to 6 percent of men). One of the most common mental health problems among women is depression. The risk may be increased by hormonal changes, such as those that occur during menstruation, pregnancy, and menopause. In addition, gender-specific stresses and cultural influences may be at play.

Anxiety Disorders: Women are twice as likely as males to have panic disorder, generalized anxiety, and specific phobias, despite the fact that men and women have obsessive-compulsive disorder and social phobias at comparable rates.

Post-Traumatic Stress Disorders (PTSD): Violence against women, particularly sexual and gender-based violence, is more common than it is for males, and this may result in post-traumatic stress disorder (PTSD). Abuse and childhood trauma may also be causes of mental health issues. Following a distressing incident, women are twice as likely to get PTSD as males.

Substance Use Disorders: Women who experience stress or trauma may resort to drugs or alcohol as a coping mechanism, which may result in substance use disorders.

Suicide Attempts: While women try suicide two to three times more often than men, males die from suicide at a rate four times higher than that of women.

Postpartum Depression: Some women have postpartum depression after giving birth. This condition is marked by enduring emotions of melancholy, despair, and tiredness.

Eating disorders: Women are more likely to have anorexia nervosa, bulimia nervosa, and binge-eating disorder. societal influences on one's appearance and body image may be quite influential. At least 85% of all instances of anorexia, bulimia, and binge-eating disorder are attributed to females.

Borderline Personality Disorder: The disorder known as borderline personality disorder, which is more often diagnosed in women, is characterized by erratic emotions, relationships, and self-image. Frequently, it results from a confluence of genetic, environmental, and social elements.

Body Dysmorphic Disorder: Body dysmorphic disorder is characterized by an obsession with a person's perceived physical faults or imperfections. Women who experience significant pressure to achieve cultural beauty standards may be impacted.

Relationship Stress: Women may have particular relationship difficulties, such as juggling job and family obligations, taking on caregiving duties, and managing cultural expectations in romantic relationships.

The symptoms, and therefore the therapy, might vary between men and women even when they have the same mental health diagnosis. For instance, a guy who is sad is more likely to report challenges at work, while a woman is more likely to describe bodily concerns, such as exhaustion or changes in eating or sleep patterns. Women often have issues with alcohol misuse within a few years after the start of depression, in contrast to their depressed male counterparts. Compared to males, who often find solace via sports and other pastimes, women are more prone to turn to religious and emotional outlets to combat the symptoms of depression. Men with schizophrenia are more prone to become indifferent and socially alienated, whereas women with schizophrenia are more likely to have despair and thinking impairment. Antipsychotic medications tend to work better on women with schizophrenia, and they need less personal care. Additionally, schizophrenic women report greater mood symptoms, which may make diagnosis more difficult and could need prescribing mood stabilizers in addition to anti-psychotic drugs.

Why the Differences in Gender?

What changes in the female body and brain cause these varied reactions to mental illness? The solutions might be in:

Biological factors: Changes in a woman's hormone levels have been linked to depression and mood disorders. The hormone estrogen may have beneficial effects on the brain, preventing severe symptoms in schizophrenic women during certain menstrual cycle stages and preserving the neuronal structure in the brain, which guards against some parts of Alzheimer's. On the negative side, women tend to synthesize the mood stabilizer serotonin more slowly than males, which may explain why there are more women who experience depression. It is also thought that genetics may contribute to the onset of neurological conditions like Alzheimer's in women.

Social and cultural factors: Despite progress made in achieving gender equality, women still confront barriers in terms of socioeconomic status, power, and reliance, which may aggravate depression and other diseases. Women continue to be the major carers for children, and it is estimated that

80 percent of all caring for elderly people with chronic illnesses is provided by women, which adds stress to a woman's life. Girls often experience body dissatisfaction throughout puberty, which has been related to depression. In addition, girls are more likely than boys to endure sexual abuse, and one in five women will be the victim of rape or an attempted rape, which may result in depression and panic disorder.

Behavioral factors: It has been hypothesized that women are more likely than males to disclose mental health issues, and that female patients are more likely to be diagnosed with depression and get mood-stabilizing medication as a result. Men often go to a mental health expert about their problems, whereas women are more likely to disclose mental health issues to a regular practitioner. Women, however, may experience anxiety when reporting physical abuse and violence.

It's crucial to remember that although these difficulties may impact women more often than males, they may afflict people of both sexes. Furthermore, every person's experience with mental health issues is different, and a variety of biological, psychological, and environmental variables have a role in how they manifest. In order to successfully address and manage these difficulties, it might be crucial to seek help, whether via therapy, counseling, or peer groups.

CHAPTER FOUR

SELF-CARE AND SELF-COMPASSION

Learning self-care techniques is more crucial than ever for women in these uncertain times. Recently, there has been a lot of emphasis on our ability to be resilient and keep recovering from upsetting situations. However, I've discovered that the majority of the people are no longer able to recover. Instead, they want empathy and support in order to get through yet another adversity. To take better care of ourselves, we need self-compassion and compassion for others. That means treating yourself the same way you would treat a close friend when you are going through a tough period. Self-compassion implies that when you are faced with personal faults, you are compassionate and understanding rather than blaming and criticizing yourself for your many flaws. We may enhance how we support our mind and body by pausing and observing how things are right now, without passing judgment, and by acting intelligently with a healthy dose of self-compassion when we can't do that.

The science of compassion, which is mostly based on studies in neuroscience and neuropsychology, shows that individuals who are good at managing their emotions are better able to bounce back from stress more quickly. For this reason, managing our emotions is crucial. Additionally, they are better able to profoundly hear and compassionately connect to themselves and others in that condition of calm attentiveness. A balanced response to our unpleasant emotions is necessary for self-compassion so that they are neither repressed nor exaggerated. This balanced approach enables us to understand the pain endured by others, which aids in helping us see our own position more broadly. It also results from our willingness to hold our unfavorable thoughts and feelings in conscious awareness by observing them with openness and clarity. Because we can only comprehend the emotional inclinations and triggers of others if we comprehend our own, we must first put our own oxygen mask on. Recognizing and letting go of negative thinking patterns that keep repeating themselves are necessary for effective emotion management. We may strengthen our fundamental ability to switch mental gears and be encouraged to make new decisions by learning to be "the observer" of our ideas.

Being attentive entails accepting your thoughts and emotions as they are and watching them objectively, without passing judgment or repressing or rejecting them. To feel compassion for it, we must be aware of our pain, but we must be careful not to connect too strongly with these emotions and ideas. Otherwise, we risk being caught up in them and having a bad reaction. Simply keep an objective, careful eye on them. Recognize that difficulties in life, failure, imperfection, and flaws are inevitable. Therefore, when you go through these terrible experiences, treat yourself tenderly instead of becoming upset with yourself. Recognize that sorrow and insufficiency are a part of the universal human experience. Everyone experiences it. Not only you are affected.

Self-compassion is a manner of responding to oneself as a human being rather than about performing to standards. You may endure and make improvements by showing self-care and attention when things are difficult. Self-compassion entails a profound embrace of all aspects of oneself as being a part of the human experience, including the good, the terrible, and the ugly. The tale is not accurate if there is a part of it that we cannot see or understand. And this makes it harder for us to decide what we need to do in order to advance. You'll think, *"I must do this because my future self is looking up to me and I can't afford to let her down"*, when you have self-compassion. Instead of spiraling over all the ways you're failing, when you can sit with your pain and consider what you might need to do to reach your goal—like getting up earlier for your runs or scheduling them on your phone calendar—you'll overcome obstacles and develop confidence and belief in yourself along the way. Although the change in response is small, it has a significant impact.

Writing this book as a young medic, sometimes I found it really difficult to be self-compassionate especially when I know I'd put in efforts into something which eventually didn't turn out well or didn't work out for good. With time, I got to understand one of the hidden theories of life which is, *there's a reason behind every situation or happenings.* So, each time I fail, or something didn't work out well for me as I expected, the first thing I do is to allow myself to feel the hurt but don't let it overwhelm me and I tell people the same thing each time I get to speak to them. We have to understand that not everything must work in our favor, not because the fault is ours but it's a natural phenomenon. Most times, we realize later on that, whatever didn't work out was actually for our good. If something didn't turn out well as we'd expected, it doesn't mean you didn't put in your best or make your efforts invalid. All you have to do is to allow yourself to feel the hurt because you're only human but, get back on your feet, draw out new plans and strategies to become a better you. Lastly, always remind yourself that *you've got this and you're never giving up till you become that woman you've always dreamed of.*

CHAPTER FIVE

BUILDING RESILIENCE

The ability to effectively adjust to severe or hard life circumstances is referred to as resilience.

It's crucial to remember that developing your skill set to become resilient over time is necessary. You must put in the effort to develop resilience, and you'll probably encounter obstacles along the road. It relies on your own actions and abilities (such communication and self-esteem), as well as on external factors (like your social network and the resources you have access to). Life presents us with a variety of obstacles, particularly inside the family. When life presents us with such difficulties, we are often seen scrambling for answers likc helter-skelter. Sometimes we don't care whether we are approaching things correctly or not; we just roam aimlessly, ceaselessly, and hopefully. But one thing is certain—every time we face a challenge, we consider a potential escape route or solution. But your response—your action or inaction—lies ahead after the difficult time. Here is where resiliency is useful. Even those who are tough go through stress, mental turmoil, and pain. Working through emotional pain and suffering is a sign of resilience.

Women who are resilient focus on their ability to handle difficulties, trauma, or obstacles while quickly recovering. Health issues, financial strain, work-related difficulties, business-related difficulties, problems with unstable relationships, or family issues might all be contributing factors. Life is not a bed of roses, and real-life circumstances are surrounded and entrenched in a variety of problems, some of which are unavoidable. Resilience helps us realize this. With this in mind, one is so equipped physically and spiritually to meet these difficulties, battle through them, and triumph over them. Resilient individuals, according to psychologists, seem to have an internal center of control. They think that people's activities may ultimately influence how an event turns out. While it's true that certain variables, like natural catastrophes, are beyond our control, we still need to exercise some degree of control over how we respond in these circumstances so that we can move beyond them. People that are resilient do not see themselves as victims of their circumstances but rather seek out solutions. Therefore, strong women are capable, self-assured, able to handle challenging circumstances, completely in charge of the situation, and ultimately succeed.

There are many different forms of resilience, but the most prevalent ones are: community resilience, social resilience, emotional resilience, and mental resilience.

How To Increase Your Resilience

1. Set aside time for yourself: Spend some time organizing, renovating, or reviving yourself. To help you move on, you definitely need some fresh air around you. By taking a break from your busy schedule, you may lower your stress levels and boost your immune system, giving you more stability and vigor to concentrate on the task at hand.

2. Create a network of support: You must pay attention to the cries of others around you and, if needed, provide them moral, material, or spiritual help. When tragedy surrounds you, the more people you have by your side, the greater their support will be for you, and the quicker and simpler the answer will be when difficulties arise.

3. Restructure your mentality: Your attitude is mostly to blame for your triumphs or failures, therefore you need to persuade yourself that internal fortitude, rather than the circumstances in which you find yourself, may influence your accomplishments. You may quickly go back to living thanks to your confidence.

4. Learn to adapt to any circumstance, even if it becomes uncomfortable, in order to become more resilient. Keep in mind that no ailment is ever going to go away, therefore you can never be completely at ease. Do not act as if everything is OK when you find yourself in an unpleasant situation; instead, keep in mind that this is only a temporary stage of life.

5. Always express gratitude: Gratitude is a matter of the heart; in order to express gratitude to God in any circumstance, you must be persuaded that He is your ultimate source. You will realize that you have a lot to be grateful for if you take the time to list your blessings.

Who Are Resilient Women?

A strong woman views each day as a chance to improve her life. She puts more money into herself than consumerism. She is not in competition with anybody, therefore she sensibly spends her money on things that will improve her life and the lives of her family. When the circumstances are not in her favor, she continues going until she reaches her objective rather than being imprisoned or wet by the difficulties that surround her. She utilizes her power to transform her anguish into gain rather than letting her hardship impact her. Instead of breaking under strain, she emerges even more resilient. A resilient woman perseveres even in the most trying circumstances; she draws courage from within and encourages other women to strive rather than pull them down. She makes an effort to set aside her problems and concerns and to focus on Christ. She always finds solace and serenity in Christ, knowing that although she may experience hardships, God's love endures forever.

You can tell a woman has tremendous resilience when you witness one who has experienced genuine turbulence, navigated hard seas, and emerged stronger and better. Women that are resilient persevere through adversity, gain strength from it, and even serve as an example for other women. Being able to bounce back sooner than anticipated after adversity is a sign of resilience.

The strong lady always takes her time to assess the issue and maintain her composure. She doesn't make snap judgments or lose her cool. She takes deliberate judgments and addresses the situation with maturity and prudence. A strong woman can maintain control in a tense circumstance. She doesn't feel panic for very long, but she does pray for God's help and guidance. Even though she is aware of conspiracies against her, she ignores them and continues. Strong women are often conscious of their circumstances and the feelings they are experiencing. As they give long-term solutions, they are able to regulate the problem thanks to their knowledge. When faced with a challenge, a strong woman first considers how to overcome it rather than why it occurred. She battles the threatening wind with a strong will, a good attitude, and positive energy to get through it.

CHAPTER SIX

STRESS MANAGEMENT AND RELAXATION TECHNIQUES

Your body's reaction to the everyday events that take place in your life is stress. Everybody encounters stress. Positive stress may spur women to accomplish significant accomplishments. But stress may also be harmful and destructive, having a detrimental impact on many aspects of one's life. It becomes more difficult to adjust to and manage with stress when it becomes chronic or extreme. For some women, chronic stress becomes so commonplace that it starts to seem like a regular part of life. Women are often so busy that they fail to stop long enough to consider how stress is adversely impacting them.

What signs of stress are there?

There are many signs of stress. Every woman's response to stress is different. The following are typical signs of stress in women:

1.**Physical Stress:** Headaches, poor energy, changes in sleep habits (such as sleeplessness or oversleeping), and gastrointestinal problems (such as an upset stomach).

2. **Spiritual stress:** A sense of existential crisis or emptiness, a sense of disconnection from one's beliefs or ideals, and feelings of emptiness or lack of purpose.

3. **Social Stress:** Difficulty establishing or sustaining relationships with others, isolation or retreat from social activities, interpersonal problems, or tense conversations.

4. **Occupational stress:** More tardiness, worse job satisfaction, trouble focusing or making choices at work, burnout, or overwhelming sensations.

5. Emotional Stress: Changes in mood, irritation or hostility, excessive concern or anxiety, feeling emotionally overloaded, and decreased emotional resilience.

6. Mental Stress: Increasing levels of worry or despair, racing thoughts, trouble focusing or forgetting, negative thinking patterns, and self-criticism.

Stress has several root causes. The causes of stress that are common to both men and women include concerns about money, job stability, health, and interpersonal relationships. The many roles that women play are maybe a bit more particular to them. In today's culture, women's tasks often involve caring for their families, providing for their young children or elderly parents (who are statistically more likely to be women), and working in addition to other roles. Women may have a sense of being overburdened with time constraints and unfulfilled duties when expectations to perform these tasks rise. Due to their inability to live up to both their own and others' standards, they could experience feelings of failure. Women often devote more time to taking care of the needs of others than of their own. Women who are under a lot of stress can not even be aware of their needs.

Women who experience stress over an extended period of time may have these additional health issues in addition to the stress-related health symptoms.

Depression: Women are more likely than males to have depression, anxiety, and other psychological illnesses such panic disorder and obsessive compulsive disorder.

Headaches and migraines: Women are more likely than males to get tension headaches.

Heart issues: Stress raises heart rate and blood pressure.

Obesity: Women are more likely than males to acquire weight as a result of stress.

Bowel issues: Bowel issues like irritable bowel syndrome might develop as a result of stress.

Pregnancy problems: Pregnancy is more challenging for women who are under greater stress than for those who are not.

Menstrual problems: Premenstrual condition is worse with increased stress, according to menstrual issues.

How can you better handle stress?

Healthy self-care techniques for dealing with stress may help women manage their stress. In each of these six aspects of your life—physical, emotional, mental, occupational, social, and spiritual—examine your negative stress indicators. What aspects of your life would you wish to change? What must you do to increase your potential or balance? Here are a few ideas.

1.Physical Stress

Exercise releases endorphins, which eases tension and stress in the body. Yoga, deep breathing, and progressive muscle relaxation are a few exercises that might help you relax.

2. Spiritual Stress

Women who meditate and practice mindfulness may connect with their inner selves, discover their purpose, and lessen existential stress. For spiritual nutrition, participate in activities that are in line with your particular views or go to religious or spiritual meetings.

3. Social Anxiety

Develop a solid social support system by cultivating bonds with loved ones who can help you feel better emotionally. To safeguard against social pressures and overcommitment, establish appropriate limits.

4. Workplace Stress

To preserve a work-life balance, prioritize tasks, delegate where appropriate, and abstain from overworking. Discuss issues with your managers or HR, and look for options for professional advancement.

5. Psychological Stress

Acquire knowledge about how to recognize, comprehend, and successfully control emotions. Don't repress your emotions; instead, choose healthy outlets like writing, painting, or talking to a confidant or therapist.

6. Mental Anxiety

Consider using cognitive behavioral therapy (CBT) strategies to reframe and challenge negative thinking patterns. Practice mindfulness meditation to remain in the now and cut down on mental ruminating.

Stress is a natural part of life, therefore, it's important to adapt these techniques to suit each person's requirements and preferences. A key first step in stress management is to ask for help from mental health specialists when tension becomes unbearable. Although each woman's experience in managing stress across these dimensions may be different, these tactics provide a comprehensive method of addressing the difficulties women may encounter.

Personal Wellness Plan to Help You Manage Stress

1.Self-Assessment: To begin, assess your present levels of stress and list the particular stressors in each category (physical, spiritual, social, occupational, emotional, and mental).

2. Goal Setting: Establish specific, doable objectives for lowering stress in each area. As an example, "I will practice yoga twice a week to reduce physical stress."

3. Physical Wellness: Regular exercise can enhance your physical health and produce endorphins. Eat a balanced diet that includes plenty of fruits, vegetables, and fluids. Maintain a regular sleep pattern and give sleep first priority.

4. Spiritual Wellness: Practice daily awareness or meditation. Spend time in prayer or introspection to connect with your spiritual convictions. If desired, look for a welcoming spiritual community.

5. Social Wellness: Encourage and cultivate good friendships and family ties. Recognize when to say "no" and how to establish limits. Look for social support while you're having trouble.

6. Time Management: Time management and task prioritization are essential for occupational wellness. Openly discuss work-related stresses with coworkers and superiors. Examine your options for expanding and developing your career.

7. Emotional Wellness: Become emotionally intelligent by accurately identifying and controlling your emotions. Use artistic or writing mediums to express your emotions. If necessary, seek therapy or counseling to deal with your emotional problems.

8. Mental Wellness: To maintain the present moment and lessen mental rumination, practice mindfulness meditation. CBT techniques are used to challenge and reframe negative thought patterns. Take part in lifelong learning to encourage mental development and toughness.

9. Holistic Self-Care: Plan regular "me time" for relaxing and engaging in self-care activities you enjoy. For relaxation, think about holistic strategies like massage or aromatherapy.

10. Seek Professional Assistance: If stress becomes unbearable or persistent, don't be afraid to speak with therapists or mental health professionals.

11. Regular Evaluation: Periodically assess your progress in managing stress and adjust your wellness plan as needed.

12. Support System: Lean on your support network for encouragement and accountability.

13. Mindful Living: Cultivate mindfulness in daily life by being present in each moment and savoring the positives.

Remember that self-care is not selfish; it's essential for your overall well-being.

Consistently following your personal wellness plan and implementing these helpful hints can empower you to effectively manage stress and lead a healthier, more balanced life.

CHAPTER SEVEN

NAVIGATING FAMILY DYNAMICS

There is no denying that no two families are the same. But when we get together with extended family, that's when we start to become more conscious of the dynamics inside our own families. When visiting friends' families, differences become apparent as well. Even the depictions of some of the most adored families in popular culture contradict with our personal experiences. It could make us wonder why our families can't more closely resemble what we would consider idealized models. But, for better or worse, almost everyone can agree on the importance of the notion of family because it teaches us what it is to belong to something greater than ourselves. We initially discover connections, friendships, and interactions in our families.

How do family dynamics work?

Family dynamics is a term used to describe how family members interact with one another. Culture, customs, family history, acquired skills, emotions, and the roles and hierarchy within a family all have a significant impact on them. The behaviors and connections we see within a particular family context are influenced by patterns of family dynamics.

Trustworthy friends may provide just as much assistance as family members, if not more because friends are there voluntarily and have similar viewpoints and ideals, relationships with them often experience less stress. They don't recall their intricate family history together. They are less likely to feel free to judge you based just on an affiliation. A wonderful strategy to improve your wellbeing is to surround yourself with close friends that you like spending time with.

Estrangement occurs when rifts in relationships lead to unpleasant emotions and circumstances, leading to protracted distance and little to no communication. Protecting someone from "abuse, neglect, betrayal, bullying, untreated mental illness, lack of support, destructive behavior, substance abuse, sexual orientation, choice of spouse, gender identity, religion, or political views" may be done by making that decision. It's possible to take a vacation from family members permanently or just temporarily. If you want to strive toward a future reconciliation, only you can decide that. When dealing with major, demanding issues like mourning, aging parents, chronic sickness or disease, children moving out of the house (empty nest), etc., it will help to be patient, accepting of the changes, and working through any challenges together.

Honest, open communication entails having frequent, in-person conversations where family members respect one another by hearing out one another's viewpoints. Safe and secure environments are those in which family members engage with one another with a sense of emotional well-being. Family members who are aware of others' needs freely express their affection and show it by making loving and considerate gestures and doing caring acts. A family that values and respects one another believes in giving their other family members a sense of value and appreciation. Addressing conflict means cooperating to find a solution or make repairs so that relationships within the family are solid and resilient.

How To Deal With The Dynamics Of The Family

Family relationships are always evolving. Learning more about how to handle some of the difficulties that unavoidably occur as part of family dynamics might be helpful.

Division of labor: Making sure that no one individual is solely responsible for keeping the home running smoothly. Every member of the family should pitch in to keep the house in order. It's important to understand the distinctions between discipline and punishment. With discipline, you are guiding someone's learning and teaching them a new behavior. The learner is the main emphasis. When you use punishment, you are instilling dread in the target behavior. The individual administering the penalty is highlighted. Understanding what someone is saying by paying close attention to their words is a talent that may be developed. Don't give in to the impulse to interject and provide suggestions.

Establish sound boundaries: Boundaries assist family members agree on what subjects are appropriate and inappropriate to discuss in the context of the family unit. Setting limits during encounters and discussions enables certain information to remain private while also helping to maintain uniqueness. Everyone should work to provide a secure environment where members may talk about issues while upholding boundaries and allowing for openness and honesty within those limits.

The value of independence: A person's health and wellbeing may greatly benefit from acknowledging and promoting the need for people to grow into and express their independence while still being cherished family members. When it's essential, letting go and cutting connections might provide someone the space they need to handle a difficult circumstance on their own. While family members may provide support and direction, recognizing that someone has to discover their own path can improve the family dynamic.

Divorce: When relationships fail, divorce may result. Everyone engaged may have a terrible and distressing experience. It will be crucial to explain the family dynamic to everyone, but notably to the younger generations as the woman in charge.

In order to prevent upsetting the dynamics of the family, family members should educate themselves on harmful behaviors that lead to conflict. Watch out for tactics like manipulating, placing blame, threatening, criticizing, dismissing, being extreme, dramatizing, etc. Naming the behavior is a technique to say that you won't participate in or keep up conversations or encounters that display these traits. Despite the complexity of family relationships, our family experiences shape and affect how we interact with others and the rest of the world throughout our lives. If family dynamics become exceptionally challenging, consider seeking the assistance of a mediator or family therapist.

Navigating family dynamics is an ongoing process that requires patience, understanding, and effort from all family members. By fostering healthy communication, setting boundaries, and promoting empowerment, women can play a vital role in creating a harmonious and supportive family environment.

CHAPTER EIGHT

FRIENDSHIPS AND SUPPORT NETWORKS

Female connections are necessary for your growth and wellbeing as a woman. They can give your life color and act as a support network you would not otherwise have. The delight and comfort of community and companionship are hard to match, and cultivating and maintaining a strong, empowering group of female friends requires conscious effort. We ladies are aware that no other kind of friendship can compare to the relationship between women. Whether it's a long-time childhood buddy or a recent acquaintance who simply understands you, these connections may be immensely potent sources of pleasure, support, and happiness. Your stress levels and self-esteem may both benefit from having close female connections. The following are some major ways that female friendships may be significant and advantageous:

Help on an emotional level: One of the most significant advantages of female friendships is the help they may provide. Having a buddy who can provide a sympathetic ear, a shoulder to weep on, or a reassuring embrace may make all the difference when you're going through a trying moment. According to research, social support may make people feel happier, less stressed, and even less depressed.

Validation: Having friends that accept and value you for who you are might assist to increase your confidence and self-esteem. It might be simpler to trust ourselves and make choices that are consistent with our beliefs and priorities when we feel heard and understood.

Shared experiences: Making connections and building friendships with friends may be done in large part through sharing experiences. Whether it's visiting a new restaurant, enrolling in a class, or taking a vacation, sharing experiences with others helps create memories that will last a lifetime.

Accountability: It might be simpler to keep on track and hold ourselves responsible when we have friends who share our objectives and ambitions. Having a companion who is on the same page may assist to give encouragement and support, whether it's maintaining an exercise schedule, eating healthfully, or taking up a new pastime.

Joy and laughter: Laughing and having a nice time with friends may assist to relieve tension and improve mood. Numerous health advantages of laughter have been shown, including enhanced heart health and decreased pain and inflammation.

Believe it or not, having close connections might really help your immune system work better! A specific antibody that aids in infection resistance was shown to be present in larger amounts in women with strong social networks, according to one research.

Strong female friendships take work to establish and keep up, and neither is true for everyone. It requires time, effort, and the readiness to be openly vulnerable and truthful with one another. If you are having trouble with this, here are some pointers to get you going:

Friend-wise, Act How You Would Like To Be Treated: One of the many benefits of friendship is that it gives us a place to feel comfortable that we may not find with our families or in romantic relationships. You must be kind and respectful to your friends since they have decided to love and support you without being required to. Love, support, and wholesome relationships are fostered through sincerity, compassion, thoughtfulness, and transparency. You need to be a good friend first if you want to develop good connections. Show up for your friends—to birthdays, significant occasions, or to expose a cheating lover. You should be present for your friends and be prepared to take whatever action necessary to improve their life. Your pals should have the assurance that you are always on their side by crying with them when the time comes and helping them get up after they have been down too long. When your friends make mistakes, be the sort of friend to gently correct them so that they will assist you in getting your bearings when necessary. Building and sustaining a strong, supportive network of friends requires reciprocity, and friends may benefit from one another's advice on how to improve.

Step Up In Your Game: Your buddies should be a secure place where you can discuss everything with them and they should be able to do the same with you. Anyone who is judgmental, a patriarchal princess, or who slut-shames her pals is not someone anyone wants to be friends with.

You must concentrate on being accepting of others and willing to learn and grow if you want good friends who will accept you for who you are. Keep in mind that we support both the rights and the wrongs of women, and even if you are unable to communicate your wrongs with others, you should be able to do so with your friends.

Be Open And Honest: sincerity and trust are the foundations of true friendship. Share your worries, uncertainties, and difficulties with your pals without hesitation. They may have gone through comparable circumstances and may provide insightful advice and support.

Make Time For Regular Gatherings: Whether it's a weekly coffee date or a monthly book club, making time for your friendships a priority in your schedule may assist to strengthen those bonds. Nothing except shared memories and experiences may bring people together. Try new things with your pals since sharing even the negative experiences may make them memorable. Go out, have a fantastic time, snap plenty of photos, and watch out for one another. At the end of the day, someone must break into an emotional drunk speech about how wonderful friendship is and how much you love one another.

Engage In Active Listening: It might be tempting to speak about ourselves a lot when we are among friends. But it's crucial to keep in mind that successful friendships are mutually beneficial. Put your phone away, actively listen to your friends, engage in conversation, and show a genuine interest in their life.

Discover Common Interests: There are many topics that may cause people to connect, and these connections can grow into strong friendships. A friendship might grow in other ways if the two people have interests in the same things, such as music, literature, fashion, or artists. Take an interest in the things that your friends find appealing.

Celebrate Each Other's Accomplishments: Friendships which suffer from jealousy and competitiveness are said to be toxic. Instead of embracing toxicity, make an effort to recognize and appreciate your friends' successes. This will assist to strengthen your relationships and create a more upbeat, encouraging atmosphere.

Even after you meet a man, treat your female friendships seriously and not as filler. Relationships with friends are just as vital as those with lovers, and they should be handled as such. It is crucial that you give back to your community because it will support you in ways that no one else would. Make an effort, organize friendship outings, spend time with your pals, and don't prioritize guys above your friendships. Don't be the friend who stays away from her pals the moment she meets a guy; it's not lady-like.

All in all, behave like a girl's girl, be self-assured and compassionate, and you'll probably draw individuals who share your opinions and beliefs. But don't forget to guard your personal space and use discretion. Although female friendships are wonderful, there may always be exceptions. Consider friendship red signals to be just as severe as romance red flags, and run from any indication of evil. Female friendships have many advantages beyond merely having a companion to speak with over coffee. These connections may enhance our wellbeing in a variety of ways, ranging from lowering stress and anxiety to enhancing the immune system and self-esteem. So don't be afraid to reach out, be open, and express your gratitude for the crucial role that the women in your life play in your life if you want to develop stronger relationships with them.

CHAPTER NINE

ROMANTIC RELATIONSHIPS AND MENTAL WELLNESS

Although it has long been believed by social scientists that men's and women's mental health are more closely related to intimate social relationships, new research shows that there are no gender differences in the benefits of marriage and drawbacks of single status when taking into account the different ways that men and women express their emotional distress. These results support the notion that the significance of intimate relationships for both men's and women's mental health has increased. For non-marital love relationships among the present cohorts of young people, these tendencies may not be visible, however.

Healthy relationships require work and compromise from both sides and entail open communication, honesty, trust, and respect between partners. There is no power disparity. Partners share choices, accept each other's freedom, and are free to act independently without fear of repercussions. There is no stalking or unwillingness to let the other partner leave if or when a relationship ends.

Many women claim that despite their best efforts, they are unable to maintain their relationship. Some claim they were unaware of the relationship's decline at the time. But in fact, women are aware. Even though we know when something is awry, we often attempt to persuade ourselves that it will pass. Or that he'll put out effort if he wants it to succeed, instead of following their intuition, and this causes us to often dwell in denial. Don't be hesitant or self-conscious. Follow your instincts and bring up suspicious situations when you can. The only way to get over relationship difficulties is via communication with your spouse. Yes, there are instances when the greatest relationship advice for women is to let it go and go on, but more often than not, the relationship goes stale because you and your spouse aren't talking about the important issues. You are choosing to suppress your emotions and letting the relationship suffer as a result. From the moment you make first contact with a possible lover, trust your gut. Is he often late and continually making up lame excuses? Don't expect him to suddenly be on time when you need him to go someplace essential since he doesn't respect your time. When you sense anything that doesn't sit well with you, pay attention to your gut reactions. This is crucial guidance for single women. You'll be astonished by how amazing your relationship may be once you learn to start believing in yourself.

The road to finding the right partner for you is paved with many incorrect steps, and relationships may be challenging. Not usually do you receive exactly what you see. You neglect to look for a better guy for yourself in your efforts to learn how to be a better woman in a relationship. In order to maintain a happy and successful relationship, society lays a lot of emphasis on how one should behave. But because every individual is unique, they may not be able to live up to these constricting standards. The finest relationship advice for all women is to be genuine while showing consideration for their mate. It won't be effective for very long to pretend to be someone else. You will eventually get upset with your inability to be genuine in your relationship. Furthermore, your relationship might become poisonous if you don't respect and care for your spouse. These are necessary for a relationship to progress and improve over time.

For a relationship to be successful, a woman must act with compassion toward both her own emotions and her partner's. If you put too much pressure on yourself, it will make you miserable and lead to relationship issues. In the same vein, your spouse could feel trapped and evaluated by you if you are overly harsh with them. By giving them room to be honest and vulnerable, you should attempt to strengthen the trust in your connection.

As long as she takes care of herself and ensures that she is devoted to the relationship she is in, a woman will be excellent in a relationship. Her degree of irritability and the attachment she has with her partner may deteriorate if she is not prepared to be in a relationship. In addition, you need to be in a relationship with a person who is also open and dedicated to being in one. They can solve their issues piecemeal as long as both sides are prepared and ready to negotiate a solution.

How Can I Be A Resilient Woman In A Relationship?

Have A Personal Life

Getting overly enmeshed in her partner's world and forgetting to pursue and sustain her own hobbies is the worst relationship error a woman can make. While being a pair is nice, it's equally critical to preserve your individuality and sense of self. Maintain your contacts outside of the relationship while pursuing your own interests.

Beginning a new relationship with a guy does not require you to give up all of your interests and reduce them to match those of your partner. Even the happiest relationships may lose their spark when they spend too much time together.

Make sure to keep doing the things that made you the person your spouse fell in love with. You had a life before he did. Women should remember that men like independent women, so don't let your hobbies lapse simply because you are in a committed relationship. Although you may be madly in love with one other, your life shouldn't end just because of that. Leave your buddies behind for him. If you don't want to give up your massages and start playing golf, don't. Have some autonomy and a distinct identity. Because if you don't, the relationship will become monotonous and routine.

Give Him Healthy Space

Having needs and pursuing may coexist. Sadly, a lot of women engage in this behavior. And you may not even be aware of it. "Chasing" may take many different forms; it could include overt stalker-like conduct like phoning him 100 times a day. Or, it might be more subtly expressed, such as the fact that you are always the one to make contact, indicating that you are more interested in him than he is. You're being needy if you want to communicate with him by text or phone all the time and essentially believe the world revolves around him. Needy conduct is oppressive to others, particularly males. You believe that these actions will keep him close to you, but they actually have the opposite effect and drive him away.

Please don't feel the need to contact, text, or email him often to see how he's doing. Give each other some space, particularly if your relationship is only just getting started. Men place a high value on having a sufficient amount of healthy distance in a relationship. When he is thinking about you and pondering what you are doing, that breathing room is where all the magic takes place. He won't have anything to imagine if you update him often. This important piece of relationship and love advice is often ignored.

Love And Prioritize Yourself

There are a lot of women who lament that they either can't find the proper guy or that they constantly seem to attract jerks who treat them poorly. You probably don't love yourself enough, that's why. Only as much love as you feel for yourself will you be able to attract. Consider all your positive attributes and make the decision to accept yourself as you are right now. If you love yourself, taking care of yourself will come naturally. This entails making an effort to maintain good health, get adequate sleep, get massages, take bubble baths, or even go out with the ladies. You won't have anything left to offer until you take care of your soul in other ways outside your relationship.

Many women have the false belief that if they win the favor of others, they will thereafter be loved. The opposite is true, as you can see! If you give a lot of yourself out, a lot of people will take advantage of you. Instead, make an effort to strike a balance between selfishness and selflessness. You'll attract someone who won't love and respect you if you don't love and respect yourself first. The first step is to love yourself. You can't beat yourself up figuratively and want respect from others. You better believe that people will notice this. You will find the sort of relationship you desire after you learn to love and respect yourself.

Self-Care

Women are born nurturers, and caring for others, especially our spouses, gives us a lot of joy. But in a partnership, a woman has to cease sacrificing her own contentment and calm. Prioritize your physical, mental, and emotional well-being. The importance of self-care cannot be disputed. Make self-care activities that support your mental and physical health a priority. You may maintain your resilience by engaging in regular exercise, a good diet, meditation, and relaxation exercises. Set and maintain appropriate limits in your relationship. Be frank about your boundaries and let your partner know what they are. Self-respect and self-care are often where resilience starts. Do your best to include good self-care practices. Don't limit your position as a woman in a partnership to being the only caretaker.

A Guide to Compromise

It's an issue if the other person in your relationship consistently pushes back and refuses to see things your way. Stubbornness is one thing. However, failing to compromise is a certain way to end yourself in trouble. Shutting up and listening—really listening—are essential skills for mastering the art of compromise. Be sympathetic and try to see yourself in your partner's position. You'd be amazed how frequently it benefits you to be understanding. Frequently, your spouse will imitate the conduct you model. Relationships tend to grow when you treat others like you would want to be treated, albeit not always. Make sure your spouse is happy, but also that they are happy with you. Relationships are reciprocal in nature.

Don't Assume, Communicate!

Talk about the positive, negative, and humiliating things. Describe your expectations in detail. You set yourself up for passive-aggressive behavior and recurrent disappointment if you are evasive about what you want and then get upset or resentful when your spouse doesn't fulfill your hidden expectations. Inform your spouse so they may decide whether you want to go to dinner on Saturday night. Never assume; rather, enquire, be specific, and discuss one another's requirements. Successful couples are skilled at listening to their partners' needs and conveying their own.

Drama is a bad way to encourage your spouse to accomplish anything, however. Your dramatics will just make him less interested in you. The turmoil isn't beneficial for you either since you could like being a resilient woman in a relationship.

Express And Speak Your Mind

When I say, "Speak your mind," I mean you should do it slowly and deliberately. Neither happy nor negative emotions should be repressed. Release them. Any issues you are facing may be discussed with your partner. Try to think of yourselves as a team and work to find solutions together. You deserve to be treated with respect and listened to. Nobody truly enjoys a fight. The majority of individuals don't, yet maybe there are a few that do. As a result, individuals often adopt an avoidance strategy. This is unsuccessful. Problems will accumulate if you put them off for years on end. Once they've accumulated for too long, you'll wake up 25 years from now and never be able to sort through them all.

Don't Settle For Bare Minimum

There are far too many individuals who worry about being by themselves. They probably don't love themselves enough to fight for what they deserve because of this.

The compromise is "Mr. Good Enough for Now." And after a short period of time, they find themselves unhappy. While you will never find "Mr. Perfect," you shouldn't give up looking for "Mr. Right" either. Nothing wrong with being by yourself! It may even feel pretty liberated. You are not required to make concessions to anybody. You are free to do anything you want, whenever you want. Nobody is there to answer to. You may improve your self-awareness and endeavor to be a better person. Don't hurry things, no matter how excited you are to be in a relationship. The reveal is where the true fun is. Before increasing your degree of closeness, take some time to get to know one another. It will be much more enjoyable when you get there.

Be Certain That The Relationship Is What You Want

Conduct periodic mental health check-ins: Do you feel joyful when you're with him, or do your dates leave you feeling agitated or angry? Do you enjoy yourself when you consider him? Does he treat you, your job, and your interests with respect or does he disparage them? The most crucial question is: Does he appreciate you and what you bring to his life? Do you appreciate him and the things he brings to your life?

Never Accept Abuse Of Any Kind

Abuse is more than simply being beaten or physically assaulted. Abuse may be physical, psychological, or emotional. Even while physical wounds may heal, mental and emotional wounds take significantly longer to mend. Therefore, if he attempts to minimize, disparage, or gaslight you, don't put up with it. That really ruins the transaction.

Break Up If Necessary

If you feel that none of your relationship-improvement attempts are working, don't put off the inevitable. Yes, being alone might first seem frightening, but it's better to be alone than to be in a relationship that makes you unhappy and saps your energy. You don't want to learn how to treat men well and then realize fifty or sixty years later that you squandered your love on someone who didn't value what you had to give.

CHAPTER TEN

SETTING GOALS AND ASPIRATIONS

Women's life goals will put you on the proper track to achieve your definition of success! Setting goals for yourself as a woman is crucial for obtaining success and happiness in all facets of life.

The aims, wishes, and accomplishments you have for your life are known as life goals. Personal, professional, and other areas of our lives pertaining to our employment, relationships, health, personal development, and economics may all be included in our life objectives. Having objectives may give you a feeling of direction and inspire you to go for your aspirations.

Setting and accomplishing life goals may provide people a feeling of direction, satisfaction, and purpose. existence objectives may inspire people to go for their aspirations, face their obstacles head-on, and build a meaningful and content existence. A higher education degree, a career in a specific field, a trip to a new country, bettering one's physical health and fitness, forging close bonds with family and friends, giving back to the community, achieving financial security, having a child, or leading a meaningful life are some examples of life goals.

Women might have short-term or long-term goals in life, and they may change over time just as you do. Setting values-aligned, attainable objectives and working toward them with commitment, persistence, and adaptability are the key. Women have unique hurdles that force us to maintain our concentration on whatever it is we are trying to accomplish. We should make extremely precise objectives that assist us in realizing our potential and fulfilling our life's purpose in addition to repeating affirmations on a regular basis and believing that they will be effective.

THINGS EVERY WOMAN SHOULD AIM FOR

This is a fantastic chance to consider your objectives for the next year. How are you going to work harder this year and the next year to achieve the objectives you've set for yourself? Here are a few examples of objectives any woman needs to establish for herself. You may start right now and will soon be well on your way to becoming your most vivacious, healthiest, and best self.

1. GO AFTER WHAT YOU WANT

This should be every woman's top objective! Any desire you may have, now is the time to pursue it. Follow it and give it your all, whether it's establishing a company, developing a talent, relocating close to the coast, launching a clothing line or jewelry collection. Your intuition is constantly active and serves as your guidance when you're a woman. Use your future vision as a guide to pursue your heart's and soul's desires. If you keep a notebook or calendar, you may want to start writing down your objectives once a month so that you never lose sight of what you want to do and what motivates you the most to get out of bed in the mornings. Finding motivation and a sense of purpose in life may be attained through pursuing your aspirations. Additionally, it may assist you in maintaining concentration and maximizing your time.

2. GO IT ALONE

A fantastic approach to see other cultures and discover more about yourself is by traveling the globe. It might also give you a fresh outlook on life and provide you with new chances. Our time on this planet is finite. See and experience as much of the globe as you can. You can go someplace you'd never think of going and yet have your mind blown; you don't even need to travel very far. By experiencing things from many angles and learning to completely trust yourself while facing all of your concerns, traveling alone helps you mature and become a more well-rounded person. Traveling will help you relax and unwind in addition to expanding your mind and exposing you to new experiences. Why not take a train ride or travel to the next town on your next weekend? Try something new and reward yourself! The more activities you engage in that push you outside your comfort zone, the better.

3. PLAN TO SAVE MONEY

A lady needs to SAVE! Always start setting money aside for significant purchases. Whether it's for a trip, a fancy purse, or a down payment on a home. Make a promise to yourself and follow your spending plan. When you commit to it for even a few months of the year, you'll be astonished at what may happen, and after the year is done and your goal is achieved, you'll be able to reward yourself with anything you really desire!

Taking charge of your life and feeling powerful may both be accomplished by being financially independent. You may have greater flexibility to follow your ambitions and exercise independent judgment as a result.

4. BEGIN INVESTMENT

Did you know that women tend to invest less than men? In order for women to feel economically equal and independent, investing is crucial. By investing, you may prepare for retirement and achieve your financial objectives more quickly! We believe that investing should be a ritual similar to any other that we do. Make it a habit to save money for your future, no matter how little. Learn as much as you can about investment, and consult a financial planner.

Developing a new talent may boost your self-assurance and feeling of achievement. Additionally, it could provide you fresh chances in both your personal and professional lives. A wonderful life goal for a woman is to acquire a new talent, whether it be a language, an instrument, a culinary technique, or something else different. A fantastic approach to take charge of your destiny and change the world is to launch your own company. In addition to being a terrific source of cash, it may make you feel proud and accomplished. It's also a goal that empowers women since it allows you to be your own boss and make your own choices.

5. SUBSCRIBE TO A MASTERMIND OR INVEST IN A LIFE COACH

While investing your money is crucial, long-term rewards come from investing in yourself. You are definitely setting yourself up for success when you invest in a life coach or even a self-help course, whether it's to get rid of your blocks or phobias, build closer relationships, learn how to be a better CEO, or take a mastermind or marketing course. When you join a mastermind group, you may not only make new connections with individuals who share your interests but also get inspiration and support from complete strangers to help you stay on track to reaching your objectives. Having someone lead you step-by-step so you can become the strongest woman you can is really empowering.

6. DEVELOP A DISCIPLINE

You must practice greater discipline if you want to accomplish anything. That calls on you to establish and adhere to a rigid plan and deadlines for yourself. To start your day off well, establish a disciplined morning ritual. Starting with meditation, exercise, rising at the same time each morning, taking vitamins, and creating aims and affirmations for the day are all good places to start. Then, make a monthly overview and note all of your significant events and deadlines. However, this is often insufficient to keep you on track; for this reason, make detailed daily overviews that will help you remember to meet these deadlines and schedule your day hour by hour.

7. FORM A CHAIN

To ensure that you truly do what you set out to do, establish a chain for yourself.

According to a widely used approach, if you take only 30 minutes every day to do one modest task, you will be astounded by the progress you accomplish. Maybe you over complicated your objectives this year; maybe you need to get back to the fundamentals. Exercise for 30 minutes each day. 30 minutes a day should be spent blogging. Spend 30 minutes per day learning a new language. You may achieve your objectives more quickly by making a chain of commitments to one item each day. Make a note in your notebook of each day, and keep the pattern going.

8. COMMIT TO SELF-CARE

Spend money on weekly or monthly massages, therapy sessions, energy work, spray tans, hair appointments, or a spa day to take care of your body. Your capacity to love yourself more deeply and your confidence increase as you make self-care investments. Additionally, your body, soul, and mind will appreciate you for it! For women, having better health is a major life objective. You may feel and look better by eating a balanced diet and exercising often. You may be less stressed and more productive with its assistance.

Finding a profession or vocation that you really like may significantly improve your life. It's important to discover a fulfilling and passionate activity for yourself. This might include finding a new position or moving up in your existing organization. Finding a work you love is a fantastic life goal for a woman and a crucial aspect of self-care, regardless of gender.

You need time with your family for your emotional and physical wellness. You may develop enduring memories and strengthen connections as a result.

9. VIEW MORE

Every billionaire is an avid reader! You should read more to aid your development. Read biographies, self-help books, business books, cookbooks, books on health & wellness, and even periodicals. You should read as much as you can on the topics that interest you or that you wish to learn more about. Get some fresh insights and new information. Reading is a great method to expand your mind, learn new things, and develop your communication abilities.

10. HELP OUT

A woman should prioritize changing the world in her life goals. It might be as simple as giving back to your neighborhood or as grandiose as founding a non-profit.

Why not lend a hand at a local charity or nonprofit in your community? Working as a volunteer in a hospital or a homeless shelter may teach you valuable lessons and increase your empathy and compassion for others. Volunteer at the animal shelter near you! You not only give back to the world and your neighborhood, but you also help others out of pure altruism. You will always get this gift from the cosmos in some mystical manner. Giving from the goodness of your heart also results in a higher sense of satisfaction.

11. FALL IN LOVE WITH YOURSELF

Every woman feels pressure to find love, but what if society encouraged us to love ourselves before we found someone else? Imagine if we prioritized ourselves and treated ourselves with the same respect that our predecessors did their spouses. Redirect all the love and effort you would devote to a relationship to loving yourself instead! We stop looking for love to fill our hole when we are completely in love with ourselves. And since no holes are being filled, love that we discover is as pure as it can possibly be. Finding purpose in your life and being motivated may both be attained through pursuing your passion. Additionally, it is an act of self-love. You may do more in both your personal and professional life with its aid. Leaving your comfort zone is a crucial component of personal development. It might encourage you to take risks and broaden your horizons. A fantastic life objective for a woman is to push herself beyond her comfort zone, whether it be through speaking in front of an audience or taking on a new project.

We develop confidence when we embrace who we are. When compared to insecurities, confidence is calm. Learn to love yourself through developing more self-assurance. Love is compassionate, loving, trusting, having no expectations, being present, and unconditional. Be nice to yourself, have faith in yourself, let go of your own expectations of you, be in the moment with yourself, and have unconditional love for your body!

CHAPTER ELEVEN

CAREER AND FINANCIAL WELL-BEING

In the difficult world of today, it is critical to understand the particular financial difficulties that women experience and how those difficulties affect the financial security of women. Our ability to seek more education, training, and interests as well as the quality of our social interactions and relationships are all greatly influenced by our financial situation. And in terms of money, women face additional challenges that their male counterparts do not. In addition to women having a higher chance of being financial abuse victims, they also have to deal with obstacles like the economic gender gap.

Prior until recently, men's wants and concerns were overlooked in favor of the specific requirements and worries of women when it came to financial preparation and security. Even while the financial services sector has made significant strides in redressing this imbalance, older women and younger generations are still feeling the repercussions of that historical neglect. To narrow the gap between men and women in terms of financial stability, a lot more effort has to be done.

Each of us encounters circumstances and setbacks that are unique to us during our existence. It is clear why education is essential to ensuring women's financial health is preserved when one considers the extra financial demands and disadvantages that women experience throughout their whole lifetime.

The average pension savings disparity between men and women is greatest among those approaching or in retirement, but it also exists among younger generations.
There are several causes for the ongoing disparity in pension benefits between men and women, with the gender pay and income difference being the most prominent. Women are also more likely to pause their careers to care for children or

other family members, which interferes with their capacity to work and accumulate savings for retirement.

It is difficult for all generations to close the pensions gap. Women who are nearing retirement need guidance and assistance in increasing their savings while making the most of their current assets. Younger and mid-career women, however, need empowerment and education in order to make financial choices that will put them on the path to better stability in the future. An awareness of how much money they would need in retirement to maintain their preferred level of life is an excellent place to start with this education and empowerment.

It is evident that the present cost-of-living problem has a significant negative effect on mental health and productivity levels. Women are also making bigger financial sacrifices to meet the demands of rising living expenditures in order to ensure their future.

These cost-of-living constraints are added to the long-standing financial difficulties that have impacted the financial security of women.

A major barrier to reducing the gender gap is the underrepresentation of women in the financial sector. Investing early in life is one of the most reliable ways to accumulate assets for retirement. Women must be financially empowered at every stage of their life in order to address this challenge, and the workplace is a key setting where this empowerment may occur. In developing just and equitable solutions that promote and increase women's wealth throughout their financial journeys, responsible employers may play a significant role.

There are various reasons why women's careers and financial security are crucial:

1. Economic Empowerment: Women who are financially independent and have successful occupations help a society's economy as a whole. Women themselves, as well as their families and communities, gain from this.

2. Gender Equality: A key component of gender equality is achieving financial and professional parity between the sexes. The equality of opportunity, rights, and respect for women is ensured.

3. Reducing Poverty: Women often make up a significant share of individuals who live in poverty, therefore empowering them financially may help lower poverty rates. The level of life for women's families often rises when they have access to higher-paying occupations and financial resources.

4. Health and Well-Being: Women's access to better healthcare, education, and living circumstances for themselves and their family is made possible by financial stability, which enhances their general well-being.

5. Role models: Women who are successful in their chosen industries may provide inspiration for younger generations, encouraging them to follow their dreams and challenge gender norms.

6. Social and Political Participation: Financially independent women are more likely to participate in social and political activities, promoting their rights and bringing about beneficial society reforms.

7. Long-Term Stability: Women who have career and financial planning have a feeling of long-term stability, which lessens retirement and future fear.

8. Creativity and Diversity: A diverse workforce, including women's viewpoints, may foster more creativity and problem-solving, which is advantageous to society as a whole.

9. Worldwide Development: According to the Sustainable Development Goals of the United Nations, empowering women economically is acknowledged as a major factor in sustainable development on a worldwide scale.

In essence, women's career and financial security are very important on a large scale. It is essential to creating societies that are more just, affluent, and progressive.

CHAPTER TWELVE

FINDING PURPOSE AND FULFILLMENT

Although each woman will have a unique life purpose, in general, a woman's primary mission in life is to build rather than to destroy. It entails leaving your loved ones with more optimism, affection, and emotional reserves than they had before. To live out your passion and provide an example for others. In addition to delivering yourself, in your authentic feminine essence, to the world, it is about finding satisfaction.

A woman is nurturing because of her maternal nature and maternal instinct. The next generation's emotional resilience is developed via this care. It enables them to go through life and get through the challenging moments they will inevitably experience with the knowledge of your unfailing love and support. You put money into the emotional resource bank for your family and friends as a woman by nurturing them! Either you strengthen them or you weaken them. Therefore, the most important duty of women in the world is to help others succeed by using their special maternal resources.

And as you probably well know, women in many nations today have been indoctrinated into believing that they are really unworthy if they aren't earning any money, don't have the standard college degree, or have no "career." It is simple to slip into this trap even if you are in touch with your femininity. But you may do the following to learn what your actual calling is as a woman:

1.) Discover what gives your life a spark.

There is always something that gives your life a spark, such as when you see someone singing or dancing. Is that what you want to do? You want to embrace it and dive in. Ask your subconscious.

2.) Discover your happy place

By identifying and continually asking yourself, "What makes me happy?" only you will be able to realize this. Finding what makes you happy and doing it is one of the uncommon methods for a woman to discover her life's purpose.

3.) Discover your passion
There is a difference between finding things that make you happy and finding things that give you a reason to live. Similar to how I love to write.

4.) What makes you happy?
If you were to ask me, the responses to my blog posts, emails, and comments from readers all over the globe would make me ecstatic because they are the fruit of the passion and purpose I have discovered in my life.

5.) What is it that you have always wanted to do? I guarantee that you are not doing it right now. Perhaps you initially wanted to be a pianist but ultimately chose

to become an architect. Even if you are making a good living and meeting all of your needs, you are not happy.

6.) What is the one activity you never get tired of?

Making meaningful art or writing never gets old for me. Poetry reading and writing never get old for me. What is it about one particular aspect of your life that gives you such a spark of energy that you can carry it out even in the middle of the night? Look into it.

7.) What do you like doing?

Do what you love and love what you do, as the adage goes. What do you believe these businesspeople are—a group of ardent individuals who took the decision to swim against the current and leave their mark simply because they love what they do and have discovered their calling in life?

8.) What motivates you?

Beautiful, forgiving, and readily inspired by everything around them, women are wonderful. So choose your environment carefully, decide what motivates you, and then do that.

9.) What sustains you?

Finding out what motivates you is one of the uncommon methods for women to discover their life's purpose; for some, this may be the love of their work, while for others, it may be the inspiration for what they do.

10.) Discover your vocation

because we all own one. The list might continue with cooking, cycling, boxing, designing, style, makeup, teaching, writing, and singing. Take your passion and examine it closely as you sit with it for a bit. Then, see what you can do with it.

11.) Make contact with like-minded individuals

Finding the correct and like-minded individuals to associate with may help you see things from a fresh perspective, learn new things, and be inspired and motivated to pursue your passions.

12.) Participate in online forums

You may opt to participate in online forums; there are many different platforms accessible. Online, there are many women-focused groups where you may interact with many women from all backgrounds and form a supportive network.

13.) Take some time to yourself

You have time to halt and think while you're alone. One of the uncommon methods for a woman to discover her life's purpose is by taking time for herself and taking command of her life in those times. In your everyday life, when you are occupied with home duties and raising children, you tend to set your ideas aside.

14.) Inquire inside oneself

You could have a lot of uncertainty and difficulty when determining your true life's mission. When you feel stuck and unable to decide what you truly want to accomplish with your life, go back to the exercise from earlier and keep asking yourself questions until you are certain of what you want. Take your time and try not to become stressed.

15.) Consider yourself

We are quick to judge others, provide input, and perhaps even condemn their decisions and way of life, but what we really need to do is assess where we are and how well we are able to critique others. It is usually simple to critique others, but it may be quite challenging to assess oneself and improve.

16.) Update your image

It's never too late to make improvements to oneself. There is always a second chance. Nothing can prevent you from pursuing your passion in life if you have a clear goal in mind, therefore never be afraid to start again.

17.) Improve your position

Continuous self-improvement is one of the uncommon methods for women to discover their life's purpose. You must live the life you want for yourself if you want to discover your purpose in life. You will remove every mental impediment, and you can only do so by realizing your entire potential.

18.) Read motivational books

Reading may inspire you and alter your outlook. Read motivating novels; they'll open your mind to new ideas and transport you to a world of limitless possibilities.

19.) Write in a diary every day.

A daily diary functions similarly to a growth, progress, and mood tracker. Writing down your everyday emotions allows you to reflect on your ideas and keep track of your feelings and activities.

20.) Set and accomplish objectives, one objective at a time

Yes, one objective at a time, and that one is much too achievable. Only you are aware of your capability and skill; set objectives based on that knowledge rather than on the opinions or expectations of others. Setting priorities and deadlines helps you take control of your life. Your life's mission becomes more clear to you.

Also, I want to emphasize that you shouldn't allow your marriage to prevent you from developing; instead, create rules and redefine marriage. Your life begins when you want it to; it is occurring right now; all you need to do is halt, take stock, and take control.

Never compare your achievement to others' success metrics or your life to theirs. Everyone experiences some degree of unfairness in life, but the only thing that counts in this situation is how we handle those unjust situations and continue to fight. Discovering your life's purpose can help you wake up every day feeling amazing. Until then, take a deep breath and give thanks for

all the tiny things in your life. Be careful.
Remain secure and rational.

CHAPTER THIRTEEN

RECOGNIZING WHEN TO SEEK PROFESSIONAL HELP

Women are more likely than males to have a number of common mental diseases, including sadness and anxiety. And regrettably, women can go months or even years without getting help for a mental disorder. Women are more likely than males to have a number of common mental diseases, including sadness and anxiety. And regrettably, women can go months or even years without getting help for a mental disorder. This occurs sometimes because they don't even recognize how serious the issue is until their lives start to spin out of control. Due to their busy lives nowadays, women may mistakenly attribute their symptoms to stress or burnout when they truly have a more serious issue.

How do you know, then? How can you tell whether you are just stressed out? Or, how can you tell whether you may be dealing with a mental disease that needs to be identified and treated by a mental health expert? Let's examine some typical indicators of mental illness to assist you in determining this.

Symptoms Specific To Women

Mental illness affects women in a somewhat different way than it does males. In particular, males are more likely to externalize mental diseases like drug misuse, drunkenness, and antisocial behaviors, while women are more likely to internalize mental illnesses like sadness and anxiety.

(I) An internalizing mental disorder is one that makes a person withdraw from others. It often causes retreat, rumination, loneliness, and depressive emotions. When this symptom is coupled with other circumstances, women who find themselves withdrawing from life and internalizing their feelings should think about the likelihood of a mental illness. Additionally, compared to males, women often have greater physical signs of mental illness.

(II) Symptoms of mental illness might include headaches, nausea, stomachaches, persistent discomfort, and high blood pressure. Other physical indicators include poor sleep, weight changes, fatigue, or reduced sex desire. A doctor should always be consulted when experiencing physical complaints. Women who encounter unexplained physical symptoms, however, may think about the potential of an undetected mental disorder after a medical diagnosis has been ruled out.

(III) Difficulty coping with daily life
Sometimes a decline in functioning is one of the earliest indications of mental illness. This may manifest as poor academic achievement, subpar job performance, inability to fulfill obligations, trouble

managing stress, or issues in personal relationships.

(IV) Mood and emotional changes

Another key indicator of many mental diseases is unexplained or unusual changes in mood or mood swings. A sad mood, sensations of exhilaration, excessive energy, a lack of emotion, or feelings of indifference might be signs of this. As an alternative, a person could feel uncontrollably guilty, afraid, ashamed, or angry.

(V) Poor cognitive function

These could include issues with memory, trouble focusing, or moments of bewilderment. Such disturbing cognitive symptoms should be investigated for potential mental disorder.

(VI) Dangerous or unusual actions

unsafe behaviors may result from mental illness, including extravagant spending, unsafe sexual conduct, and drug and alcohol experimentation. When a person has both a drug or alcohol addiction and another disease, such as depression or PTSD, this is known as a dual diagnosis.

(VII) Breaks with reality

Psychotic disorders are characterized by breaks with reality. These might seem as paranoia, hallucinations, delusions, or a feeling of disassociation from reality.

Steps You Can Take

Take the time to investigate this if you or a loved one shows any indicators of a potential mental illness. Find a women's treatment facility so that you may be evaluated and diagnosed by a qualified mental health expert.

You may manage a mental health condition with a variety of therapies. Your therapist could suggest therapies like dialectical behavioral therapy (DBT) for bipolar illness or borderline personality disorder or cognitive behavioral therapy (CBT) for depression or anxiety. Remember these warning signals and keep an eye out for them in your life by taking the time to do so. Sometimes, the easier it is to treat and manage a mental illness, the sooner you notice its start.

CONCLUSION

In conclusion, embracing your mental health journey is a powerful and transformative endeavor for women. It's a path toward self-discovery, self-compassion, and personal growth. By acknowledging the importance of mental health and prioritizing self-care, we can overcome challenges, break down barriers, and thrive in all aspects of life. This journey not only enriches individual lives but also has a ripple effect, fostering a more empathetic, supportive, and inclusive society. So, let us champion the journey to mental well-being as women, recognizing that in doing so, we empower individuals and create a more resilient, compassionate world for all.